The Role of the United Nations

SIMON ADAMS

FRANKLIN WATTS
LONDON • SYDNEY

First published in 2004 by Franklin Watts
96 Leonard Street, London EC2A 4XD

Franklin Watts Australia
45-51 Huntley Street
Alexandria, NSW 2015

Series editor: Rachel Cooke
Editor: Andrew Campbell
Series design: White Design
Picture research: Diana Morris

A CIP catalogue record for this book is available from the British Library.

ISBN: 0 7496 5418 X

Printed in Belgium

Acknowledgements:.
Amalvy/AFP/Popperfoto: 26b. Pascal Beaudenon/Sipa/Rex Features: 13t.
Luc Delahay/Sipa/Rex Features: 12b. Jamie Drummond/Christian Aid/
Still Pictures: 15b. Mark Edwards/Still Pictures: 5b, 20t.
Romeo Gacad/Reuters/Popperfoto: 22b. Goran/Reuters/Popperfoto: 25b.
Monika Graff/The Image Works/Topham: 28t. Paul Harrison/Still Pictures: 16b.
Henryk T. Kaiser/Rex Features: 17r. Ton Koene/Still Pictures: 15t.
Heathcliff O'Malley/Rex Features: 29b. Kevin R. Morris/Corbis: 23t.
Gerard & Margi Moss/Still Pictures: 21b. Shehzad Noorani/Still Pictures: 7b, 19t.
John Parkin/Reuters/Popperfoto: 8t. Popperfoto: front cover, 4b, 13b.
Laurent Rebours/Reuters/Popperfoto: 27t. Rex Features: 11t.
Sayed Salahuddin/Reuters/Popperfoto: 14t. Gilles Saussier/Still Pictures: 26t.
Harmut Schwarzbach/Still Pictures: 8b. Mike Segar/Reuters/Popperfoto: 6b.
Sipa/Rex Features: 24t. Topham Picturepoint: 18b.

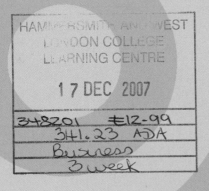

CONTENTS

THE UNITED NATIONS (UN) *is the most important international organisation in the world. Almost every country in the world is a member, and at times of crisis they look to the UN to prevent war and keep the peace. But while the UN aims to encourage co-operation and stability, it often finds itself at the centre of controversy – either for what it does, or does not do.*

US Secretary of State Edward Stettinus signs the UN Charter in San Francisco on 26 June 1945, watched over by President Truman (second left).

FOUNDING THE UN

On 7 December 1941, the USA entered the Second World War (1939–45) on the side of Britain and the USSR against Germany, Japan and Italy. US President Franklin Roosevelt and British Prime Minister Winston Churchill met soon afterwards to co-ordinate their war efforts. On 1 January 1942, they issued the Declaration of the United Nations, calling for a "more permanent system of general security".

Over the next three years, detailed plans for this new organisation were drawn up. On 26 June 1945, just after the end of the war in Europe, leaders of 50 Allied nations met in San Francisco to sign the UN Charter. The new organisation came into existence on 24 October 1945, and met for the first time in London on 10 January 1946.

THE UN CHARTER

The UN Charter states that: "We the peoples of the United Nations are determined to save succeeding generations from the scourge of war, which twice in our lifetime has brought untold sorrow to mankind." The charter sets out three main aims: maintaining international peace and security; developing friendly relations between states; and encouraging countries to work together to solve economic, cultural, social and humanitarian problems. It also expresses hope for the equality of all people and the expansion of basic freedoms.

HEADLINE NEWS

Today, 191 countries belong to the UN – Taiwan and the Vatican City are the only states that are not members. The sheer size of the organisation, and its involvement in many global issues, are enough to make it "newsworthy". However, the problems the UN faces in achieving its aims – for example, finding ways to prevent war, or ensuring that all nations work to protect the environment – guarantees it a place in the world's spotlight.

FACING THE ISSUES

The UN is not the first world institution that has tried to promote stability and trust. At the end of the First World War (1914–18), US President Woodrow Wilson urged all nations to set up an international organisation, called the League of Nations, to preserve world peace and settle any future disputes by agreement. The League was not a success, because the USA eventually refused to join and many other countries, such as Germany and Japan, left when they were criticised. The League failed to prevent the Second World War, and then collapsed.

➡ The UN building in New York. The building, completed in 1952, is the organisation's permanent headquarters.

THE UNITED NATIONS IS A VAST and complex organisation, employing almost 9,000 staff in its headquarters in New York and many more in various political, humanitarian and military missions around the world. Because the UN is responsible for so much, it is divided into five main parts.

SECRETARIAT AND GENERAL ASSEMBLY

The work of the UN is controlled by the Secretariat, which employs translators, lawyers, press officers, secretaries and many others to make sure the organisation runs smoothly. The Secretariat is headed by the Secretary-General (see box). Another key part of the UN is the General Assembly, which works like a parliament: every country is represented by one seat, no matter how big or small they are. The assembly discusses policy and decides how the UN spends its budget. It can also hold emergency sessions to discuss issues of immediate importance, such as to approve war against in Iraq in 1991. To reach a decision, two-thirds of the member states (128 out of 191) must vote in favour.

→ *Secretary-General Kofi Annan has done much to raise the status of the UN in recent years, and to increase its effectiveness in dealing with its vast workload.*

GET THE FACTS STRAIGHT

There have been seven secretary-generals since the UN was founded, from Norway, Sweden, Myanmar (Burma), Austria, Peru, Egypt and Ghana. Kofi Annan, the present Secretary-General, was born the son of a chieftain in Ghana, West Africa, in 1938. He was elected to the job in 1997, after 35 years' work for the UN, including posts as the High Commissioner for Refugees and the Assistant Secretary-General for peacekeeping. As Secretary-General, he has had to deal with many problems, notably the global spread of AIDS, the continuing problem of Palestine and the war in Iraq. In 2001, Annan and the UN received the Nobel Peace Prize for their work in promoting peace. In the same year, the General Assembly appointed him to a second term of office, from 2002 to 2006.

SECURITY COUNCIL

The most important part of the UN is the Security Council, which has responsibility for maintaining peace and security around the world. The council has five permanent members – the USA, Russia, China, Britain and France – and ten temporary members, elected for two years by the General Assembly to represent each continent. The five permanent members can veto, or vote against, any measure they dislike, causing it to fail. Members use this powerful weapon as a last resort – since 1990, the veto has only been used 13 times.

TWO OTHER PARTS

The two remaining parts of the UN are the International Court of Justice at The Hague in the Netherlands, where countries can take legal action against one another, and the Economic and Social Council. The Council, which has 54 members elected for three years by the General Assembly, co-ordinates the UN's efforts to improve the living standards of poor people around the world. It looks after the work of 15 UN agencies and other linked organisations (see box right).

GET THE FACTS STRAIGHT

Here are some of the main agencies and organisations the UN runs or is linked to:

- Food and Agriculture Organisation (FAO)
- International Atomic Energy Agency (IAEA)
- International Monetary Fund (IMF)
- UN Children's Fund (UNICEF)
- UN Conference on Trade and Development (UNCTAD)
- UN Development Programme (UNDP)
- UN Disaster Relief Organisation (UNDRO)
- UN Educational, Scientific and Cultural Organisation (UNESCO)
- UN High Commissioner for Refugees (UNHCR)
- UN Population Fund (UNFPA)
- World Bank
- World Health Organisation (WHO)

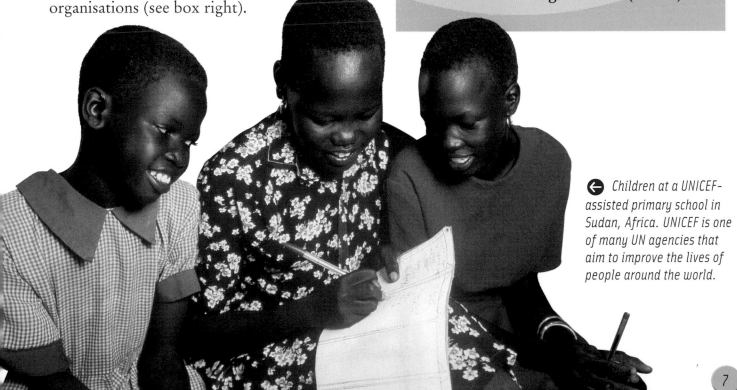

← Children at a UNICEF-assisted primary school in Sudan, Africa. UNICEF is one of many UN agencies that aim to improve the lives of people around the world.

WHO PAYS?

BECAUSE IT IS SUCH A HUGE *organisation, the UN requires large amounts of money if it is to work efficiently and deliver the programmes and policies its member states have voted for. But problems in raising funds means that the UN often has to struggle to meet its costs.*

THREE-WAY SPLIT

The UN currently spends its money in three ways: on its regular budget, which covers most of its activities; on the two international tribunals trying war crimes that occurred during the 1990s' conflicts in Rwanda and former Yugoslavia; and on peacekeeping missions. Its budget is always set in US dollars. In 2002, it spent $2,535 million (about £1,580 m) on its regular budget, $200 m (£125 m) on the tribunals, and $2,100 m (£1,315 m) on peacekeeping, a total of $4,835 m (£3,020 m).

GET THE FACTS STRAIGHT

Top ten contributors to the UN in 2002

USA	22%	$1,060 m	(£665 m)
Japan	19.268%	$930 m	(£580 m)
Germany	9.493%	$460 m	(£286 m)
Russia	6.283%	$300 m	(£190 m)
France	6.283%	$300 m	(£190 m)
UK	5.38%	$260 m	(£160 m)
Italy	4.992%	$240 m	(£150 m)
Canada	2.573%	$125 m	(£78 m)
Spain	2.488%	$120 m	(£75 m)
Australia	1.64%	$80 m	(£50 m)
Rest of world	19.636%	$950 m	(£595 m)

⬇ *UN workers unload food supplies in Sudan as part of a famine relief operation. Such operations cost the UN a lot of money.*

5Y-TAJ

UN

→ *In 1996, the UN paid for lorries to return refugees in Rwanda to their homes. The operation saved many people from being killed by their enemies.*

FAIR SHARES

When the UN was set up, it was agreed that its members would share its costs. Each state pays a different amount according to its wealth – rich nations, such as Britain or France, pay far more than poor nations, such as Algeria or Congo, regardless of population or size. Every member state has to pay a minimum of 0.01 per cent of the total budget, which in 2002 was about $483,000 (£300,000).

UNFAIR SHARES

The UN relies on its members to pay their contributions on time, otherwise it will run out of money and be unable to fund all its work that year. However, many states are slow in paying, or refuse to pay altogether as a form of protest. During the 1960s and 1970s, the USA objected to UN criticism of its involvement in the Vietnam War and other issues, and began to hold back some of its payments. By 1996, the USA owed the UN more than $1,590 m (£990 m). Other nations failed to make payments because they could not afford them, or because they considered them unfair.

CRISIS POINT

This situation has still not improved. By 30 September 2002, member states owed $2,400 m (£1,500 m) of the total UN budget for 2002. In order to survive, the UN raids those of its budgets that are in credit, but this makes its overall finances very shaky indeed. Many people think the situation has reached a crisis point, which can only be overcome by countries paying up.

WHAT DO YOU THINK?

- When you join an organisation, you accept its rules. Do you think that a member state has the right to refuse payments if it objects to what the UN does, or if it is criticised by the UN?
- Do you think that UN members should be forced to pay their contributions?
- The USA pays almost one-quarter of the total UN budget. Do you think this is fair? Think of the advantages and disadvantages to the USA in paying such a large proportion of the budget.
- If you were in charge of an organisation and a member refused to pay membership fees, what would you do?

DIPLOMACY

THE UNITED NATIONS WAS BORN at the end of the most destructive war in human history, in a century marked by warfare and conflict. The UN charter made one of the organisation's main aims the development of friendly relations between the nations of the world.

On 29 September 1960, the USSR's leader Nikita Krushchev famously interrupted a speech at the UN General Assembly by the British Prime Minister Harold Macmillan. Tempers sometimes flare at the United Nations.

JAW-JAW

The UN is, in effect, a world parliament, where diplomats from rival nations can discuss issues they disagree about, and perhaps reach agreement. In 1954, British Prime Minister Winston Churchill remarked that "to jaw-jaw is always better than to war-war". Talk can prevent conflict, and a number of disputes have been settled at the UN in this way.

A WORLD OF DIFFERENCES

The main problem faced by the UN is that its member states are not equal. Some, like the USA and Britain, are rich nations with large armies; others, such as most African states, are poor and defenceless. Most members are democracies, but a few, such as Myanmar (Burma), are governed by unelected leaders, who deny the rights of their citizens. Most nations in Europe and America are Christian; the Arab nations are Islamic. These and other differences mean that there is often little in common between member states, making it difficult to reach agreement.

UNION OF SOVIET SOCIALIST REPUBLICS

SETTLING DISPUTES

If a dispute breaks out between rival nations, the UN can intervene. It can send the Secretary-General or another high-ranking official to act as a mediator (someone who encourages talk and co-operation between all sides in a conflict), or offer to host talks between the two sides. The UN has long been involved in mediation efforts on the Mediterranean island of Cyprus, attempting to end the hostility between the Greek and Turkish Cypriots. In 2003, UN Secretary-General Kofi Annan arranged face-to-face talks between the leaders of both groups.

FACING THE ISSUES

During the 1960s and 1970s the UN rarely applied sanctions, but by the 1990s it used them far more frequently. It relied on economic and arms sanctions to force co-operation from Iraq, Liberia, former Yugoslavia, Somalia and Rwanda, among others. Sanctions worked better in some situations than others. They persuaded Libya, for example, to hand over two of its citizens who were accused of bombing the US plane that exploded over Lockerbie, Scotland, in 1988. In 1993, however, when a military coup seized power in Haiti, most observers thought that force rather than sanctions should have been used to restore the civilian government. The sanctions denied food and medicine to more than 100,000 Haitians, many of them children.

An Iraqi child suffering from malnutrition and other illnesses. In the 1990s, many people criticised UN sanctions for restricting the import of medicines to Iraq.

SANCTIONS

If a country refuses to co-operate, the UN has another option: to impose sanctions. These are restrictions on a country's activities, including banning its leaders from travelling abroad, preventing sales of its goods to other countries, and setting up a land, sea and air blockade. This option can be effective, but it can also hit the wrong target. During the 1990s, sanctions against the Iraqi leader Saddam Hussein did little to make him respect the UN's wishes, but did kill many Iraqi children, who were denied life-saving drugs because trade with Iraq was restricted.

KEEPING THE PEACE

THE UN CHARTER STATES THAT

the main purpose of the UN is to promote international peace and security through diplomatic, economic or military action. Sometimes, if diplomacy fails, the UN has no choice but to send in troops. UN soldiers may try to prevent a conflict from spilling over into violence, or stop more fighting breaking out.

↘ *UN peacekeeping troops and armoured personnel carriers in former Yugoslavia, mid-1990s. UN peacekeepers tried to keep the warring Serb, Croat and other groups apart.*

THE SECURITY COUNCIL

If one country is attacked by another, it can ask the UN for help. The Security Council will quickly meet, and attempt to end the fighting through diplomacy or possibly sanctions. If these do not work, it can decide to authorise the use of force by member nations, or send in UN troops. As the UN does not have its own army, these troops come from its member nations.

AUTHORISING FORCE

The Security Council can require member nations to fight on behalf of a country in order to repel its attackers, as the USA and 14 other nations did in South Korea from 1950 to 1953 to prevent North Korea taking it over. The UN can also approve member states to liberate a country from an occupying power. In 1991, the US-led coalition of 29 nations freed Kuwait, after Iraq had invaded it the previous year.

⬆ *A UN peacekeeper stopping and searching cars for guns and other weapons – one of many roles that peacekeepers undertake.*

PEACEKEEPING

Peacekeeping – the use of soldiers to prevent violence without fighting themselves – is an extremely difficult part of the UN's activities. It is necessary when civil war threatens a country and the two sides have to be kept apart, as in Cyprus in 1964, or when a bitter war has just ended, but there is a risk that fighting could start up again, as in Bosnia from 1995 and Afghanistan from 2002 (see pages 14–15).

MANY JOBS TO DO

The role of UN peacekeepers can vary enormously. They might intervene in a battle to separate the two sides, hunt down war criminals, act as a police force, and make sure no side breaks any ceasefire agreement. They might also set up a temporary government and supervise elections, or help to rebuild a country by repairing roads, restoring power and water supplies and reopening schools and hospitals.

GET THE FACTS STRAIGHT

- Between 1948 and 2003, the UN has been involved in 57 peacekeeping missions. In 2003, 15 of those missions were still in operation, in countries such as Sierra Leone, Ethiopia, Georgia, Kosovo, Afghanistan and East Timor.

- In 2003, 36,987 military and police personnel were serving in UN operations, drawn from 89 countries; a further 10,090 civilian personnel were also involved.

- Since 1948, 1,798 people have been killed in UN peacekeeping operations. The estimated total cost of all missions since that date has been approximately $44,612 m (£27,730 m).

➡ *UN peacekeepers wear blue berets or helmets, to mark them out as non-combatants.*

Casefile : AFGHANISTAN

↗ *Many houses like this one in Kabul, the Afghan capital, were destroyed when the US-led coalition overthrew the Taliban in 2002.*

THE ROLE OF THE UN PEACEKEEPERS

is more than just keeping the peace. Often, they have to rebuild an entire country ravaged by war, famine and disease. Since 2002, peacekeepers have been involved in the reconstruction of Afghanistan in Central Asia, which has been in a state of almost continual turmoil since 1975.

A BLOODY HISTORY

In 1975, Islamic forces known as the Mujahideen took up arms against the Afghan government. Four years later, Soviet troops invaded, and a decade of civil war followed. In 1992, the Mujahideen regained control, but in 1996 they were overthrown by a more extreme Islamic group, the Taliban. In 2001, a US-led coalition overthrew the Taliban because of their support for the al-Qaida terrorist network.

A HELPING HAND

Since 2002, the UN has been extremely active in Afghanistan. UNICEF has encouraged 3 million children back to school, installed 5,600 supplies of safe drinking water and supplied food and medicine to millions of people.

AFTER THE WAR

Today, Afghanistan is littered with the remnants of war. Up to 150 Afghans are killed each month by stepping on unexploded shells and landmines. UN mine-clearers are working to remove some of the 10 million landmines littered around the countryside. Above all, the UN is encouraging some of the 6 million refugees who fled the fighting to return from exile in Pakistan, Iran and elsewhere. Nearly 2 million have now come back, helped by the UN with food, cash and survival kits of blankets, plastic sheeting, buckets and soap.

An Afghan girl receives a vaccination. Since 2002, UNICEF has vaccinated 11 million Afghan children against measles .

This man is detecting landmines, part of the UN's effort to clear Afghanistan of 10 million such weapons.

FACING THE ISSUES

In 2003, one of the main problems facing the new government of Afghanistan is that its control is limited to the capital city, Kabul, and the surrounding areas. The rest of the country is in the hands of local warlords, one of whom has called for a holy war against the occupying UN peacekeepers, while another owns an army of 25,000 soldiers and is enforcing rules and regulations similar to those of the deposed Taliban regime. A third warlord, Fahim Khan, commands 18,000 of his own troops, but is also the national Minister of Defence. Disarming these local warlords and their private armies is a huge and difficult task for both the Afghan government and the UN peacekeepers.

SOCIAL ISSUES

THE UN CHARTER DEMANDS *much of its member nations. It requires them to work for higher standards of living, including jobs, health care and education for people all over the world – not just for the citizens in their own nations. Some people think that these demands are too high.*

HOW THE SYSTEM WORKS

The UN achieves its social aims through various specialist agencies. Some of these, such as the UN Children's Fund (UNICEF) and the UN Development Programme (UNDP) are part of the UN itself; others, such as the UN Educational, Scientific and Cultural Organisation (UNESCO) and the World Health Organisation (WHO), are intergovernmental agencies related to the UN. All report to the UN's Economic and Social Council (see page 7).

IN AGREEMENT

Much of what these bodies do is non-controversial. WHO, for example, promotes health research around the world, monitors epidemics, evaluates new drugs and advises on health standards. One of WHO's aims is to ensure that all children are immunised against major diseases. In a remarkable success, it managed to eradicate smallpox from around the world by 1980, and by the early 21st century it was on course to get rid of polio as well.

← *A doctor takes a swab from an African child, part of the successful WHO campaign to eradicate the deadly riverblindness disease.*

FACING THE ISSUES

The UN is concerned that the rising world population – now more than 6,000 million people – will lead to environmental catastrophe. In 1994, the UN International Conference on Population and Development agreed to fund an ambitious programme to lower population growth. Its efforts have had mixed results. In Iran, the UN-supported family planning programme has been a success, but in the USA, anti-abortion groups persuaded the government to withdraw funding from the project in case it was being used to pay for abortions. All agree that population control is necessary, but religious and moral objections make it difficult to achieve.

IN DISPUTE

However, the UN's social agenda often causes disagreements. One controversial issue is whether the UN should focus on providing basic human needs, such as clean water, or whether it should it act to promote equality, justice and an all-round improvement in the quality of life for every citizen in the world.

HARD QUESTIONS

Many people think the UN should take the latter, more ambitious option. They think that it should achieve this by tackling the main causes of world poverty, such as a lack of basic amenities, low international aid and unfair trade practices. But this would require huge amounts of money from richer nations, and there is no agreement that the interests of poor countries are more important than those of the rich.

➜ *The UN is increasingly concerned about the world's rising population, and its effect on the planet's fragile environment.*

HUMAN RIGHTS

ON 10 DECEMBER 1948, the UN approved one of the most important documents of modern times, the Universal Declaration of Human Rights (UDHR). The declaration set out, in its words, "a common standard of achievement for all peoples and all nations", although few of the countries that signed it have lived up to the document's high ideals.

WHY HUMAN RIGHTS?

When plans for the UN were drawn up during the Second World War, basic human rights, including the right to life itself, were being denied to millions of people living under Nazi or Japanese occupation. The UN Charter therefore included an obligation on all states to promote human rights, but did not spell out what these were. The UDHR, drawn up three years after the war, was much more detailed. It declared that people everywhere have such human rights as the right to life, the right to live without oppression and the right to equal freedom of opportunity.

GET THE FACTS STRAIGHT

Eleanor Roosevelt (1884–1962), the wife of US President Franklin Roosevelt, was closely associated with the UDHR. In 1946, she chaired the UN Commission on Human Rights and played a key role in writing the declaration. But Eleanor displayed her passion for human rights long before the UDHR, campaigning for equal rights for women and ethnic minorities. In many states in 1930s USA, segregation (separation of black and white people) was widespread. Whenever Eleanor visited a public meeting at which black and white people had to sit on different sides of the room, she placed her chair in the aisle between the two groups to demonstrate her opposition to segregation.

🔽 *Eleanor Roosevelt was one of the main authors of the UDHR and an inspirational campaigner for human rights around the world.*

🡥 *A Bangladeshi boy making cigarettes. In 1989, the UN approved the Convention on the Rights of the Child, to protect children's rights and restrict child labour.*

SIGNING UP

That same year, 1948, the General Assembly approved the UDHR, although eight members abstained: Saudi Arabia, South Africa and the USSR and five of its communist allies. Two further documents agreed in 1966 – the UN Covenants on Economic, Social and Cultural Rights and on Civil and Political Rights – spelled out the intentions of the original declaration in more detail. More than a hundred other human rights agreements have also been approved, dealing with everything from the rights of refugees to banning torture and genocide.

ENFORCING RIGHTS

Although many countries may have signed the Universal Declaration of Human Rights and other documents, their desire to enforce human rights often remains questionable. Some nations have ignored a number of the articles in the UDHR, or do not recognise its authority in their law courts. Other states recognise certain bits of the declaration, such as Article 5, which bans torture, but not others. However, by 2000, 45 countries had allowed their citizens to petition the UN Human Rights Committee if they felt their country had violated the Covenant on Civil and Political Rights, while European nations have set up their own Court of Human Rights to which their citizens have access.

⬈ *Congested traffic in Bangladesh, as elsewhere in the world, causes pollution and increases global warming.*

ONE OF THE MOST URGENT ISSUES

the UN has to deal with is the threat to the environment. Many people agree that, as a world organisation, the UN should deal with issues that affect the future of the planet. Unfortunately, there is less agreement as to how these issues can be solved.

GROWING CONCERN

When the UN was founded, it concentrated on the economic recovery of countries ravaged by the Second World War, and helped poor nations develop their own industries and fight poverty and ill-health. Concern for the environment was restricted to protecting endangered species and conserving nature. But in the 1960s, the UN began to realise that unlimited economic growth and rapid industrialisation was damaging the world's environment. In 1968, the UN held the first in a series of international conferences on the environment, starting with one on the biosphere – the part of the Earth that sustains life.

THE EARTH SUMMIT

In 1992, the UN held its largest environmental conference – the Earth Summit in Rio de Janeiro, Brazil. The summit dealt with issues as diverse as sustainable development, biotechnology and hazardous waste. It also agreed a plan called Agenda 21, which outlined ways to clean up the environment and encourage development in industry and transport that did not harm nature. In 1997, another major conference at Kyoto in Japan continued the work of the Earth Summit.

FACING THE ISSUES

In 1997, UN members approved the Kyoto Protocol, which aimed to reduce global warming by cutting greenhouse gas emissions by 30 per cent by 2010. But in 2001, US President George W. Bush pulled the USA out of the Protocol because he said it would harm the US economy, even though the USA produces 25 per cent of all such gases. The gains made by carrying out the Kyoto agreement are not, in any case, that big: they would only delay a temperature rise for six years. The global cost of meeting the targets, however, is vast – the cost to the European Union alone could provide every person in the world with access to education, basic health and fresh water. While global warming is a remote threat to most of us, a lack of fresh water can kill a person in days.

WHOSE PLANET?

Although there is widespread agreement that the world's nations must act together to tackle the environmental crisis facing the planet, there is huge disagreement as to which countries should do what. The UN is often caught in the middle of these disagreements. For example, industrial pollution contributes to climate change, but poor and developing countries like India and China need more industries in order to provide jobs and income for their vast populations. They do not see why they should be denied the industrial wealth that rich developed countries already have. On the other hand, nations that do make an effort to improve the environment can be angry when other countries refuse to reduce the waste produced by their factories, farms and transport systems.

A low-lying atoll (coral island) in the Pacific Ocean. Atolls – and island countries such as the Maldives – could disappear if global warming continues to raise sea levels.

THE UNITED NATIONS is only as strong as its members allow it to be. If the world's major nations support it, the UN can do much to achieve its aims. But if those countries, especially one of the five permanent members of the Security Council and particularly the USA, oppose or ignore it, then the UN suffers.

LONG-TERM RELATIONSHIP

The UN began life in the partnership of the USA and Britain during the Second World War, and the USA has been a leading member of the UN ever since. The founding UN conference was in the US city of San Francisco, its headquarters are in another US city, New York, and the USA has always given the UN more money than any other country (see pages 8–9).

BAD FEELINGS

However, the relationship between the two has not always been good. US dissatisfaction with the UN led it to withhold funding during the 1980s. Part of that protest was that the USA accused UNESCO – the UN's cultural organisation – of favouring less-developed nations against the USA and other western countries. In 1984, the USA left UNESCO in protest, and has yet to rejoin. Britain also left in 1985, although it rejoined in 1997.

A US soldier in Iraq. The USA has the most powerful army in the world and can act alone in any war.

AMERICAN POWER

Since the end of communism in the USSR and its subsequent break up in 1991, the USA has become the world's only superpower and by far the strongest member of the UN. Because of its unrivalled power, the USA needs the UN less than before and can act independently. Many people in the USA have always disliked the UN because they believe that no international organisation should have the right to tell the USA what to do.

➡ *UNESCO-sponsored restoration work on the ancient royal palace at Angkur Thom, Cambodia. Unlike other UN members, the US government no longer contributes to the work of UNESCO.*

FACING THE ISSUES

The USA was born after colonists rebelled against British rule in a revolutionary war between 1775 and 1781. The country's constitution, approved in 1787, makes it clear that the USA stands for liberty and freedom and is against oppression and tyranny. Above all, it states that the USA is a free country that sets its own laws. Over the next 200 years, many immigrants arrived in the USA, fleeing oppression in their home countries. They brought with them a belief in the American dream of liberty, prosperity and freedom. Many Americans therefore distrust the UN, because they fear it has set itself up above national governments and has the authority to tell the USA what to do.

ACTING ALONE

The USA's difficult relationship with the UN can be seen in many of its decisions since the late 1990s. The USA has refused to accept the international ban on the use of landmines agreed in 1997, as well as the UN targets set at Kyoto in the same year to prevent global warming (see pages 20–21). It also refused to join the new International Court of Criminal Justice (ICCJ), set up in 1998 to try suspected war criminals. The USA fears that the ICCJ might be used to try US soldiers and civilians, and is busy negotiating agreements with ICCJ members to grant immunity (a guarantee against legal action) to all US personnel.

IGNORING THE UN

IN MARCH 2003, the USA and Britain attacked Iraq in order to overthrow its dictatorial leader, Saddam Hussein, and disarm the Weapons of Mass Destruction (WMDs) they believed he had stockpiled. The attack did not have the support of the UN, and split the international community. Why did the USA and Britain act without the UN, and why could the UN not stop them?

⌕ *A protest in Paris, 2003, against the second Gulf War.*

WHAT DO YOU THINK?

In March 2003, the USA and Britain went to war against Iraq without UN approval.

● Were they right to do so?

● What else do you think the UN could have done to stop them? Or do you think the UN should have supported the USA and Britain?

● Saddam Hussein was a brutal dictator who killed many of his own people. Did this make it right for the USA and Britain to attack him without international agreement?

● Was force the only answer to this problem?

SADDAM HUSSEIN

Saddam Hussein became President of Iraq in 1979. The next year he launched an eight-year war on neighbouring Iran in order to seize control of a vital waterway leading to the Persian Gulf. He also persecuted the Kurdish people of northern Iraq, using chemical weapons to kill thousands of them, and punished anyone who spoke out against his rule. In 1990, Saddam invaded Kuwait, and was only forced out by a massive US-led force the following year in the first Gulf War.

UN SANCTIONS

In response to Iraq's attack on Kuwait, the UN imposed tough trade sanctions (see page 11). These were supposed to remain in place until Iraq got rid of its WMDs, including chemical, biological and possibly nuclear weapons. Iraq reluctantly agreed to co-operate, but did little to help the UN inspections teams sent to check that the weapons were being destroyed.

SECOND GULF WAR

After the terrorist attacks on the USA on 11 September 2001, US President Bush named Iraq as part of the "axis of evil" (alongside Iran and North Korea). The USA considered that Iraq was a threat to world peace, and that Saddam must be overthrown. British Prime Minister Tony Blair agreed, and the two countries obtained a Security Council resolution ordering Iraq to disarm. UN weapons inspectors returned to Iraq, but their progress was slow. Other members of the Security Council – in particular France, Russia and Germany – refused to support military action, but the USA and Britain decided to invade Iraq without UN backing. Australian troops also joined the US-led coalition against Iraq.

MAJOR CHALLENGE

Many observers believe that the UN now faced the gravest challenge in its history, as its two founding members had enough military force to ignore the rest of the world. However, although the US and British defeated Saddam's regime in April 2003, the task of restoring peace and order to war-torn Iraq was huge. Remnants of Saddam's regime and other groups against US intervention in the country fought a vicious guerilla campaign in which both US and British forces were killed, as were UN workers there to provide humanitarian and technological aid. As the US casualties and expences rose, it became apparent that the US would need the help of UN peacekeepers to restore long-term stability to Iraq. The US ability to "go-it-alone" was not as clear cut as it had seemed.

A statue of Saddam Hussein is pulled down in Baghdad, Iraq, in April 2003. Across Iraq, people pulled down statues of their former leader after he was overthrown.

FACING THE CRITICS

THE UNITED NATIONS HAS BEEN IN EXISTENCE *for almost 60 years, and every year it has been criticised for its actions or inaction. It is criticised for doing too much, and equally criticised for doing too little. So how successful has the UN been, and if it didn't exist, would we bother to invent it now?*

THE PLUS SIDE

The greatest achievement of the UN is, without doubt, the fact that it has survived longer than all its predecessors, notably the League of Nations (see page 5). Survival does not equal success, but it does imply that the UN has at least served a useful role in the world since 1945. Through the work of UNICEF, WHO and others, the UN has delivered massive improvements in poor people's lives through the provision of clean water, vaccination against diseases and other necessities.

⬈ Children in a slum in Mumbai, India. The UN exists to help the world's poor.

⬇ Protestors in Sarajevo, Bosnia, in 1992, demanding more UN help against the Serbians.

UNPROFOR HELP US OR GO HOME

↑ *The G8 nations, at a meeting of their leaders in France, 2003, have money and power – but could they replace the UN?*

TALK THE TALK

One criticism of the UN is that it is just a talking shop, but at times talk has prevented war. In 1962, for example, the USSR began a build-up of nuclear missiles on Cuba. Evidence presented by the USA to the UN convinced many doubters of its case, and helped to persuade the Russians to withdraw their missiles. UN peacekeepers have also played a valuable role in many conflicts, while those who suffered in former Yugoslavia and Rwanda can now see their attackers prosecuted in UN-sponsored international courts.

THE DOWN SIDE

Yet while there has been no world war since 1945, the world has hardly been at peace since then. The UN has failed to prevent, among other conflicts, the four major Arab–Israeli wars between 1948 and 1973, the lengthy Vietnam War of 1964–75, and the three wars from 1980 to 2003 involving Saddam Hussein's Iraq. Peacekeeping missions failed to prevent massacres in Bosnia and genocide in Rwanda, and were powerless in both Somalia and Haiti.

WHAT DO YOU THINK?

The UN: success or failure?

● Do you think the world is a safer place because of the UN?

● Should the UN be replaced by another organisation? If so, which one?

● In a world where the difference between nations is so great, can one organisation represent the interests of everyone?

THE ALTERNATIVE

If the UN did not exist, what would replace it? The European Union is only open to countries in Europe, while other regional bodies, such as the Arab League or the Organisation of African Unity, are too weak and divided to play much of a role. The world's major economic nations meet together in G8 (Group of 8) summits, while economic organisations, such as the World Bank, have expertise, but why should the rich nations control the world? For many, the simple answer is that the UN is not perfect, but at the moment there is no realistic alternative on offer.

 UN Secretary-General Kofi Annan addresses the UN Millennium Summit, September 2000, outlining his plans to strengthen the role of the UN in the 21st century.

THE UN HAS ALWAYS been controversial and in the news, ever since it was founded in 1945. But few countries think that it is perfect, and many have come up with ideas to improve or reform it. Concern mainly focuses on the Security Council and on peacekeeping missions, but despite the many different proposals, there is little agreement as to what changes should be made.

A CHANGING WORLD

The main change that everyone proposes is to reform the Security Council to reflect the changing world. At the moment, the five permanent members – USA, Russia, China, Britain and France – hold their seats because they were the victors in the Second World War, while the other ten members serve for two years.

SUGGESTED REFORMS

One proposal to reform the Security Council is to make other powerful nations permanent members. The British government has proposed that Japan, Germany, Brazil, South Africa and India all become permanent members, to ensure greater continuity of membership and experience. However, Mexico would probably challenge Brazil's right to a seat, and Nigeria would challenge South Africa's, making this proposal difficult to achieve. Another proposal is for the elected membership to expand from 10 to 14, making a full council of 24 members.

FACING THE ISSUES

Concern about Weapons of Mass Destruction (WMDs) getting into the hands of unstable countries like Iraq or North Korea has led Britain and others to propose the creation of a powerful new UN committee to combat the spread of weapons. The permanent committee would oversee progress in dismantling WMDs. It would also provide weapons inspectors with greater support and authority. This proposal would overcome the problems faced by Dr Hans Blix and his team of UN weapons inspectors in Iraq in 2002–03. Iraq held up the mission – although a number of long-range missiles were destroyed – which led to the invasion of US and British forces.

PEACEKEEPING PROBLEMS

At the moment, UN peacekeeping forces are assembled for each mission with troops from nations that agree to support or lead that mission. The quality of those troops varies considerably – some lack enough equipment, or are too inexperienced. For instance, in 2003 a largely Uruguayan force failed to prevent an ethnic conflict in northeast Congo that led to at least 500 deaths and created 250,000 refugees.

A PERMANENT FORCE?

To rectify this, the USA has proposed a permanent US-led international peacekeeping force, which would be properly trained and equipped to cope with any mission it was sent on. Other countries like the idea of a permanent force, but would not accept US leadership. Some would not even accept US participation in such a force. This issue is typical of many that the UN faces. It needs the support of its strongest member states, but must ensure that it represents the interests of all the world's countries. In today's world, this is no easy task.

➔ UN weapons inspectors in Iraq, 2002. Many UN members want to strengthen the role of weapons inspectors, in order to make them more effective at tracking down WMDs.

UNMOVIC-044

GLOSSARY

allies: Nations that join together against a common enemy.

budget: Summary of how much an organisation or person is going to spend each year.

charter: Formal written document setting up an organisation and specifying its roles and responsibilities.

democracy: Government by the people or their elected representatives.

developing country: A country which is developing its industry and manufacturing, but where many people still work in farming.

dictatorship: Government by a single unelected person or group of people, often acting outside the laws of the country.

diplomacy: The working out of agreements and disagreements between countries through discussion.

disarmament: The reduction or elimination of weapons.

family planning: Measures to control birth and numbers in a family, such as contraception and education programmes.

genocide: The policy of deliberately killing a nationality or ethnic group.

mediator: Someone who, during a dispute, talks to all sides in an attempt to overcome differences and seek a solution.

peacekeeping: The action of soldiers, normally neutral, to prevent rival armies attacking each other. Peacekeepers may have additional duties, from keeping law and order to distributing food to civilians.

protocol: An amendment or addition to a treaty, specifying in more detail how the treaty should be interpreted or carried out.

ratify: To formally approve a treaty, usually by a vote in parliament.

resolution: A formal statement of agreement reached by a meeting after a majority vote.

sanctions: Diplomatic, economic, military and other measures agreed by the UN against a member nation that has violated international law or failed to act upon a UN resolution.

Secretariat: The permanent administration of the UN, headed by the Secretary–General.

summit: Meeting of heads of government or other important decision-makers.

unanimous: Complete agreement; a unanimous resolution of the Security Council is agreed by all 15 members.

USSR: Union of Soviet Socialist Republics, known as the Soviet Union; the communist government that ran Russia from 1922 until it collapsed in 1991.

veto: The right to reject a resolution or action. The five permanent members of the Security Council each hold a veto on any UN resolution.

war crime: Crime committed in wartime in violation of accepted rules and customs of war.

weapons of mass destruction (WMDs): Chemical, biological and nuclear weapons capable of killing large numbers of people.

FURTHER INFORMATION

THE UNITED NATIONS

United Nations
www.un.org
The main site for the UN and its many different sections.

UN General Assembly
www.un.org/ga
Details about the General Assembly, what it does, membership and other facts.

UN Secretary-General
www.un.org/News/ossg/sg/indcx.shtml
Information about the Secretary-General, including a biography of the present office holder, Kofi Annan.

UN directory
www.unsystem.org
A guide to the UN bureaucracy.

UN AGENCIES

UN Development Programme (UNDP)
www.undp.org
Information on the UNDP's activities around the world.

UN Educational, Scientific and Cultural Organisation (UNESCO)
www.unesco.org
Read about UNESCO's Associated Schools Project Network – one of its longest-running initiatives.

UN Children's Fund (UNICEF)
www.unicef.org
What UNICEF does, where and why. Read the site's "Voices of Youth" section, for young people to discuss relevant issues in their lives and how they can take action.

UN Population Fund (UNFPA)
www.unfpa.org
Statistics on world population levels, and much more.

World Health Organisation (WHO)
www.who.int/en/
Country-by country features on health programmes, diseases and treatments.

UN ACTIVITIES

Daily news service
www.un.org/News/
Up-to-the-minute information about the UN's activities.

Economic and social development
www.un.org/esa
A guide to the UN's programmes on economic and social development.

Environment programme
www.unep.org/
The main UN website for its environmental work.

Human rights
www.un.org/rights/index.html
The main website for the UN's work on human rights.

UN High Commissioner for Human Rights
www.unhchr.ch
The website of the UN High Commissioner on Human Rights.

Humanitarian affairs
www.un.org/ha/index.html
The main website for humanitarian affairs.

Peace and security
www.un.org/peace
The main website for the UN's peacekeeping activities.

OTHER WORLD BODIES

Group of 8 (G8)
www.g7.utoronto.ca
Information about G8, with links to sites about its summits and other activities.

International Monetary Fund (IMF)
www.imf.org
The main website for the IMF.

The World Bank
www.worldbank.org
Information on the World Bank and lots of financial data.

INDEX

I don't want to say YES!

Other titles in the bunch:

Baby Bear Comes Home
Big Dog and Little Dog Visit the Moon
Delilah Digs for Treasure Dilly and the Goody-Goody
 Horse in the House I Don't Want to Say Yes!
 Juggling with Jeremy Keeping Secrets
 Mabel and Max Magnificent Mummies
Midnight at Memphis Mouse Flute
 The Nut Map Owl in the House
Riff-Raff Rabbit Rosie and the Robbers
 Runaway Fred Tom's Hats

First published in Great Britain 1998 by Mammoth
an imprint of Reed International Books Limited
Michelin House, 81 Fulham Rd, London SW3 6RB.
Published in hardback by Heinemann Educational Publishers,
a division of Reed Educational and Professional Publishing Limited
by arrangement with Reed International Books Limited.
Text copyright © Bel Mooney 1998
Illustrations copyright © Margaret Chamberlain 1998
The Author and Illustrator have asserted their moral rights
Paperback ISBN 0 7497 2810 8
Hardback ISBN 0 434 97655 5
10 9 8 7 6 5 4 3 2 1
A CIP catalogue record for this title is available from the British Library
Printed and bound in Italy by Olivotto

Bel Mooney

I don't want to say YES!

Illustrated by Margaret Chamberlain

BLue Bananas

Kitty had one favourite word.

It was No. She answered, 'No!'

to everything.

When Mum asked her if she wanted

to go to the park, she said, 'No!'

When her brother, Dan, asked her if she wanted to play with him, she said, 'No!'

7

When Dad asked her to sit on his knee and read a book, she said, 'No!'

It wasn't that Kitty didn't like going to the park, or playing with Dan, or reading with Dad. It was just that she didn't like saying, 'Yes'.

One day, Kitty and Dan were in the garden. They were playing with Copper, the cat from next door. It began to rain.

Mum called from the kitchen window, 'Come inside, you two, or you'll get soaked.'

Dan went in, but Kitty just went on riding her bike round and round in the rain.

She rode through the puddles.

She shook the rain off her hair.

She brushed

the drops off

her sweater.

She stamped in the puddles.

Then she ran
around stamping
everywhere.

STAMP
STAMP
STAMP

Kitty liked being in the garden.
There was no one out there to
tell her what to do.

I don't want to go in!

But soon Kitty was soaking.
She grew tired of playing in
the rain. She didn't like the
swishing noise of the trees.

She was bored and she was beginning to feel cold. So was Copper.

Slowly, Kitty
and Copper
walked closer
to the house.

20

Then, very slowly, they went inside.

As they crept across the kitchen, they left puddles on the floor. Mum sighed.

22

'Look at you, you're soaking wet,'
Mum said. 'You'll catch cold unless
we change your clothes.'

'Won't!' said Kitty.

Come back
here, Kitty!

'Kitty! Come here at once and
change those wet clothes!'
'No, no, no!' said Kitty
as she ran up
the stairs.

In the bedroom, Mum pushed

and pulled Kitty into dry clothes.

'You can stay in your room until tea,'
Mum said crossly. 'See if you can learn
to say, "Yes!" for a change.'

When Mum had gone, Kitty asked her bears if they liked her. But they didn't say, 'Yes'.

Kitty made
a castle with
her bricks.
She asked the
bricks if they
liked her

- but they all

fell

down.

Kitty asked her books how to say, 'Yes'.

There were lots of words inside them,

but they were silent.

The only word that came from

Kitty's mouth was a very angry, 'No!'

31

It was teatime and
Mum called Kitty
for tea. Kitty was hungry.
She walked slowly,

step

by step,

down

the stairs.

Kitty sat in her

chair and ate her tea,

but she didn't say anything.

Dan teased her. 'What's the matter,
Kitty? Lost your tongue?'

Kitty glared at him. Then she kicked at
him under the table and shouted.

She was cross with everyone and

everyone was cross with her.

After tea, Kitty lined up her toys and told them how bad they were.

Come in here now! Take off those wet clothes.

36

Dad sat in the armchair reading his newspaper. Now and then he looked up at Kitty and smiled.

'It's time for bed, Kitty,' Mum called.

'Go and kiss Dad goodnight.'

Kitty didn't want to.

Dad pretended to read his newspaper. He knew Kitty very well. He pretended he didn't want a kiss.

'Whatever you do, don't kiss me,'
he said. 'You mustn't be a good girl,
and most of all you mustn't say, "Yes!"
or I will turn into a terrible monster.'

'Now, remember, you don't want to kiss

me goodnight, do you?'

Kitty smiled for the first time that day.

And what do you think she said?

Dad started to chase Kitty.

Dad caught Kitty and gave her a big

hug. Mum and Dan laughed.

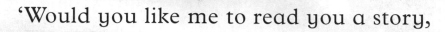

'Would you like me to read you a story,

now?' asked Dad.

And this time Kitty knew exactly what to say . . .